discover...

The
Flying Stars

discover...

The Flying Stars

Your Character and Destiny, the Chinese Way

ZAMBEZI PUBLISHING LTD

Published in 2010 by
Zambezi Publishing Ltd
P.O. Box 221 Plymouth, Devon PL2 2YJ (UK)
web: www.zampub.com email: info@zampub.com

British Library Cataloguing-in-Publication Data:
A catalogue record for this book is available from
the British Library

Typeset by Zambezi Publishing Ltd, Plymouth UK
Printed and bound in the UK by Lightning Source (UK) Ltd
ISBN-13:   978-1-903065-79-2

   Front cover background: with much appreciation, from NASA
   Content art work: ditto, from Wikipedia - various ancient Chinese artists

About the Author

Sasha became a professional consultant astrologer in 1973, but tailed off her consultancy business once her writing took off. She has written over 120 books, mainly on Mind, Body and Spirit subjects, with sales of over 6.5 million copies to her credit, and translations of some titles into a dozen foreign languages.

Having broadcast regularly all over the UK and in several other countries at times, she has also lectured widely, including festivals in various parts of the UK and Sydney, Melbourne, Johannesburg and Cape Town.

Sasha has been President of the British Astrological and Psychic Society (BAPS), Chair and Treasurer for the British Advisory Panel on Astrological Education (APAE), and a member of the Executive Council of the Writers' Guild of Great Britain.

Sasha's first husband, Tony Fenton, died of cancer and diabetes related problems. She met her second husband, Jan Budkowski, in South Africa and their first home was on the banks of the Zambezi river in Jan's country of Birth, Zambia. They married and settled in the west of England, where they now run Zambezi Publishing Ltd. Sasha has two children and two granddaughters.

Dedication
To my friend, Jackie

Acknowledgements
Thanks to Jan for all his hard work on the design of this book, and its eBook and DiskBook derivatives

Contents

Introduction

What are the Flying Stars?

The Flying Stars method is a numerology system that grew out of a long-lost and very ancient form of Chinese astrology reputed to be over 4,000 years old. You can use it to predict the future, to judge a person's character, to assess your chances for love, wealth or career success or to check out health matters. You can look at your own numbers and those of your friends.

The system is no harder to work out than any Western numerology system, and you don't need to learn or to remember anything, because everything you need is here in this book.

The system originated in China and eventually spread to Japan, and then to the West. In its various incarnations and locations, it has been known as The Nine Star Ki, Kyu Sei Ki Gakuin and The Lo Shu. The Japanese word Ki is the same as the Chinese word Chi, both meaning something like "subtle energy".

The Chinese name Lo Shu really only refers to the square numbered chart used in the system, although it's often attributed to the fortune telling technique as a whole.

In the West, the numbered chart is called The Magic Square, and that's the name that I use in this book. If you've looked into Feng Shui, you will already be familiar with The Magic Square concept. One of the fascinating characteristics of the Magic Square is that the three numbers in each row, column or diagonal add up to 15. An example is shown overleaf.

THE MAGIC SQUARE, OR THE LO SHU		
4	9	2
3	5	7
8	1	6

Astrology and the Flying Stars

Does the Flying Stars system have anything to do with astrology? It seems to have originated as such, some thousands of years ago, but some Chinese Kings and Emperors banned astrology, especially for the purpose of prediction, although they did allow Buddhist monks to study numerology. I believe the clever monks buried their astrology in code words and number systems, but, in time, the link between the movements of the heavens and their predictive systems was broken.

We know that the Flying Stars system is based on the stars popularly called the Little Bear or the Plough, and most probably also Polaris (the Pole Star) and Vega. The Pole Star sits above the North Pole, while the other stars in this group circle the pole. We know that travelers, traders and navigators still use this star group to get around, especially over long distances. This group of stars is important to those traveling from east to west and vice versa. Most long journeys in ancient China meant taking part of the trip along the Yellow and Yangtze rivers, which run from west to east. Those traveling and trading along the Silk Road to Samarkand traveled in camel trains along this special route for thousands of miles. To show how important these stars were to ancient travelers, read an account of Marco Polo's adventures, because he mentions them quite often in his journal.

Chapter One

Your Year and Month Numbers

The Flying Stars system gives accurate readings for character, and the trends for any year or any month that you wish to check out. It's much easier to than it first appears, and it's fun. Just follow the instructions and enjoy giving Flying Stars readings to your friends and loved ones.

The system is called The Flying Stars because the numbers in the system represent stars and star systems that are lost in the mists of history, but just as stars appear to move around the sky from month to month, so they appear to "fly" round the system as you use it.

Chinese New Year

The populist Chinese New Year occurs on a new moon that can fall any time from late January to late February, but Chinese astrologers use a solar year that always starts on February 4.

Thus, if you happen to have been born at any time from January 1 to February 3 inclusive, you should count your year as the previous one.

Finding Your Year Number

First of all, find your Year Number. To do this, look at the chart below and find your year of birth, then track upwards to the number at the top of the column in which your year appears:

YOUR YEAR NUMBER TABLE								
9	8	7	6	5	4	3	2	1
1901	1902	1903	1904	1905	1906	1907	1908	1909
1910	1911	1912	1913	1914	1915	1916	1917	1918
1919	1920	1921	1922	1923	1924	1925	1926	1927
1928	1929	1930	1931	1932	1933	1934	1935	1936
1937	1938	1939	1940	1941	1942	1943	1944	1945
1946	1947	1948	1949	1950	1951	1952	1953	1954
1955	1956	1957	1958	1959	1960	1961	1962	1963
1964	1965	1966	1967	1968	1969	1970	1971	1972
1973	1974	1975	1976	1977	1978	1979	1980	1981
1982	1983	1984	1985	1986	1987	1988	1989	1990
1991	1992	1993	1994	1995	1996	1997	1998	1999
2000	2001	2002	2003	2004	2005	2006	2007	2008
2009	2010	2011	2012	2013	2014	2015	2016	2017
2018	2019	2020	2021	2022	2023	2024	2025	2026

Examples

➢ If you were born in 1985, your year number would be 6.
➢ If you were born in 1990, your year number would be 1.

Finding your Month Number

To find your Month Number, look for your Year Number among the numbers that you see at the tops of the three columns in the following table:

YEAR & MONTH NUMBERS			
BIRTH DATE	1,4,7	2,5,8	3,6,9
February 4 to March 5	8	2	5
March 6 to April 5	7	1	4
April 6 to May 5	6	9	3
May 6 to June 5	5	8	2
June 6 to July 7	4	7	1
July 8 to August 7	3	6	9
August 8 to September7	2	5	8
September 8to October 8	1	4	7
October 9 to November 7	9	3	6
November 8 to December 7	8	2	5
December 8 to January 5	7	1	4
January 6 to February 3	6	9	3

Examples

➤ If you were born in 1987, your Year Number is 4, so you must look at the head of the first column.

➤ If you were born in 1965, your Year Number is 8, so you must look at the head of the second column.

➤ If you were born way back in 1931, your Year Number is 6, so you must look at the head of the third column.

Example:

Let's take an imaginary person called Emma and look at her chart so far. Emma was born on the June 9, 1984.

➤ Emma's Year Number for her 1984 birth is 7.

➤ Look at the table below and you will find the Number 7 at the top of the first column.

➤ Pick out the date that includes the June 9 and track along that row to the number in her Year Number column. In Emma's case, this is 4.

So now, we know that Emma's Year Number is 7 and her Month Number is 4.

Chapter Two

Finding your Magic Square Number

If you look at the table below, you will find columns headed with the international alphabet. Needless to say, this was never in the original system, but I've added them to help you find your way around.

Look through the numbers in the table and find the batch of three that *starts* with your Year Number and that has your Month Number in the *middle*.

THE EASY METHOD TABLE								
ALPHA	BRAVO	CHAR-LIE	DELTA	ECHO	FOX-TROT	GOLF	INDIA	JULIET
1.1.5	2.1.6	3.1.7	4.1.8	5.1.9	6.1.1	7.1.2	8.1.3	9.1.4
1.2.4	2.2.5	3.2.6	4.2.7	5.2.8	6.2.9	7.2.1	8.2.2	9.2.3
1.3.3	2.3.4	3.3.5	4.3.5	5.3.7	6.3.8	7.3.9	8.3.1	9.3.2
1.4.2	2.4.3	3.4.4	4.4.5	5.4.6	6.4.7	7.4.8	8.4.9	9.4.1
1.5.1	2.5.2	3.5.3	4.5.4	5.5.5	6.5.6	7.5.7	8.5.8	9.5.9
1.6.9	2.6.1	3.6.2	4.6.3	5.6.4	6.6.5	7.6.6	8.6.7	9.6.8
1.7.8	2.7.9	3.7.1	4.7.2	5.7.3	6.7.4	7.7.5	8.7.6	9.7.7
1.8.7	2.8.8	3.8.9	4.8.1	5.8.2	6.8.3	7.8.4	8.8.5	9.8.6
1.9.6	2.9.7	3.9.8	4.9.9	5.9.1	6.9.2	7.9.3	8.9.4	9.9.5

Example:

➤ Emma's year number is 7 and her month number is 4 we must look for a sequence that starts 7.4

➤ Now look down the column headed Golf to find her full three-number set.

➤ This is 7.4.8

Now check each of your three numbers in the next chapter (Personality) to see the various sides of your personality.

For example, Emma would look up 7, then 4 and then 8.

Chapter Three

Personality Readings

Now you can use your year number, month number and Magic Square number to assess the various sides of your personality and judge which aspects of your personality are on the outside and which are hidden away inside.

Number One

This person is a deep thinker who can brood over imagined insults. He may have strange religious or political views, and if he gets himself into position of real power he can wreak havoc, although some Number One types, like Nelson Mandela, are inspired leaders. Some are extremely restless and unsettled, following one idea after another or moving from one place to another in search of something that eludes them. Where love relationships are concerned, sex is all-important to the One type. Males in particular may confuse sex with love and they may accuse a partner who doesn't want frequent sex of not loving them enough. These people can learn by experience though, and they improve with age.

Number One people are not really attracted to business and they are not team players, neither can they cope with heavy manual work. They are best suited to careers that allow them to express their inner world, such as the arts or literature. They need work that calls upon their reserves of self-motivation, self-discipline and that gives them an opportunity to use their intellect. Therefore work in some form of research, computer programming, some forms of engineering, writing, printing, silk-screening, design, illustrating or music might suit these types. Number One people may be interested in health as a sideline, especially alternative therapies such as aromatherapy, massage or herbal medicines. Watery jobs such as fishing and the oil industry might attract. These people are good at keeping records and allocating stock, inventory and resources.

Their physical weak spots are similar to those of Libra and Scorpio, these being the kidneys, bladder, lower spine and reproductive organs. They should avoid too much salt or sugar and they should wrap up warmly in bad weather.

Number Two

Whatever the gender, these subjects are motherly personalities who take care of all those who are around them. They are excellent hosts and caterers and they ensure that their guests always have plenty to eat and drink. Number Two personalities make excellent organizers and some like to teach. They need to be part of a family or the kind of working group that feels like a family, because if they are alone for too long they become depressed. Their main fault is fussiness and too much attendance to detail. These people enjoy the countryside and they should get out into it from time to time as a kind of balm for their nerves. Number two types have the ability to attract the opposite sex quite easily, but potential partners may mistake their motives and see them as sex-objects rather than the loving family people they really are. When in a relationship, their fussiness or obsessive behavior causes problems.

In business they work well under direction and as part of a team. They love to work in fields that help others or that provide for the needs of others like nursing, catering, shop keeping (especially bakeries and grocery shops), also farming. Many Number Twos love dealing with antiques and gifts. Others lean towards the construction industry or civil engineering.

Their weak spots are their digestive organs, spleen, pancreas and stomach. They need a sensible diet without too much sugar, alcohol or coffee. The lymph system can become clogged, so gentle exercise and massage or aromatherapy does wonders for them.

Number Three

These people are courageous and idealistic and they can be a little too frank in their opinions. They are vigorous and energetic and they sometimes forget that not everyone else has their level of enthusiasm or energy. They love to come up with great ideas and they often have a number of projects on the go at once, but their hatred of detail means that these may not come to much in the long run. These ebullient folk are great fun at a party and they are extremely easy to like but too much of their company can overwhelm more sensitive souls. Even when they offend others, their ability to talk their way out of trouble or to make others laugh is a great help to them. These individuals can be very into their own appearance, buying clothes, cosmetics and visiting the beauty parlor as often as they can afford.

Number Three subjects don't take kindly to being restricted. Much of this seems to stem from their childhood, where one or both their parents tried to keep them down. In later life, they can explode in temper if frustrated. An uncaring or envious mother can undermine their confidence, giving them an insecure side to their nature, which is hidden by their brash outer manner. Sometimes the father is a bully and the mother is not strong enough to stand up to him. One survey has turned up the fact that number three women tend to be sexually abused in childhood. Where love relationships are concerned, they seem to want it all. They need an intense relationship with plenty of emotion and sex and touching. They seek an exciting partner. However, they also need their freedom, and that can cause the breakdown of one relationship after another.

Number Three people need careers that allow them to use their inventive minds. Modern industries such as website design appeal to them. They are innovative and they have the kind of mind that takes well to engineering, the electronics industry or the construction industry. They may work in the media, either on the technical side or as personalities. Writing and teaching might appeal. If in an organization, they need to be allowed to give their creativity and inventiveness free rein. They can see the big picture but they don't always know how to make it happen. When under intense pressure they blow a fuse and either have a major row or quietly quit the job and find another.

Traditionally, their weak spots are the liver and the gall bladder, so fatty foods and alcohol are not good for them, although unfortunately, this personality often does drink too much. The muscles, ligaments and tendons can also suffer so a balance between gentle exercise and rest is required.

Number Four

Number Four people tend to look cool and calm and their stubborn, determined and independent nature gives them an appearance of being in control at all times. However, this is only superficial because they can be quite tense and vulnerable inside, breaking out into moody, stubborn behavior when under intense pressure. They can see things clearly and they don't lack common sense and they know how to convince or influence others. Forward looking and innovative, these people are often ahead of their time. However, they are also sensitive to what is going on around them and they can make a great success of things when they get the timing right. They can't handle too many things at once, so they are best when working on a specific project and at their own pace. They sometimes leave things to the last minute, hence becoming labeled as procrastinators, and if someone asks them to chop and change mid-stream, they become quite worked up. The natural honesty of the Number Four type means that they put their trust in others far too easily, expecting them to have the same high standards of decency as themselves. They love music and some also enjoy art and literature. In love, they are true romantics. Their pleasant nature and arresting eyes makes it easy for them to attract potential lovers, but they are extremely choosy about who they decide to make their own. Even when a relationship does not work out too well, they try to stick it out and to put things right. If all else fails, they keep the relationship going, while looking around for someone new. They can be attracted to the wrong person for financial reasons.

These people do well in any career that requires mental agility, intelligence, patience and inventiveness. Dress design, politics, the arts and sports may attract but it's in the field of inventions, engineering and computing that they really excel. They are happiest when employed by someone who appreciates them. They may not have the vision of some of the signs but they can take a project and really make it work, improving it beyond the belief of those who thought it up in the first place. Number Four people must guard against frittering money away once they have it, so a good savings scheme is a must for these folk.

Like the Number Three type, these people should take care of their livers and gall bladders. So fatty food and alcohol should be restricted. Any gentle exercise that moves them around is good for them, so jogging, golf, cycling, walking and swimming are recommended.

Number Five

These charismatic people love to be at the center of things and they often influence those who are around them in a positive manner. They tend to be the leaders in any situation, whether at home or at work and they have to guard against being leaned upon too much by those who are less strong. They can be irritable and impatient and sometimes too blunt and inflexible, and this approach sometimes causes them to make enemies unnecessarily, which is a shame because they are actually decent, honest and loyal. Number Five people have lives that reach very high and very low and their fate and fortune can fluctuate quite wildly at times. When down, their determination and ability to work very hard brings them back up once again but they must guard against sitting back and allowing things to slide back down again. Whatever their circumstances, they have an aura of success and confidence that encourages others to put their trust in them. To some extent, this is only an outer shield because they are quiet insecure and vulnerable inside, but it may only be their loved ones who are allowed to see this side of their personality. Number Five people can attract partners easily and they are wonderful lovers, but their moodiness and occasional fits of depression can make them hard to live with. They do somehow manage to find themselves in love triangles and they can divorce, remarry and gain stepchildren as a result.

Careers for Number Five types include selling and marketing or running their own businesses. Some work in the media or as military leaders. Politics attract some, due to their love of being at the heart of important matters, while others turn the same social urge towards running a hotel or restaurant or a social club.

Health concerns are quite varied with the pancreas being a potential area to watch, with blood sugar problems high on the list, leading to heart disease and diabetes. Sometimes high blood pressure, tumors and cysts can be a problem. Also depression.

Number Six

These people have strong personalities and they exhibit great leadership qualities. Sometimes this shows itself in the sense of being a military leader or business head but in other contexts, this type becomes a strong and reliable father figure. These people like to make provision for their families, and this extends to their siblings as well as their spouses and children. These people are orderly, highly responsible and often very moral. Their lack of flexibility or ability to allow for the weaknesses of others can make them unpopular. They do have weaknesses of their own, but these are well concealed. If they fail in an enterprise, they can become quite paralyzed for a while, doing nothing much at all until something else inspires them. Sometimes their standards are too high, even for themselves and certainly for others, and this makes them critical and inwardly self-critical. These hard-working types can become rich and powerful in almost any sphere of action and some do very well in sporting and competitive activities. They take care of those who are under them. Needless to say, relationship matters can be their downfall because they may not have the time and energy to devote to these. Both sexes are great achievers and they may take on more than they can handle. Either sex can become bullies. However, if they marry later in life, once they have made their pile, they can relax and enjoy home and family life and become very caring lovers.

Careers that allow them to become leaders are the obvious ones for Number Six people, therefore the military, the police, big business and also the church would appeal. In some cases the law or transport might apply but also politics and local government work.

Health matters affect the lungs but also skin problems and headaches are possible as are heart problems and broken bones due to playing rough sports. Inner tension can lead to high blood pressure or headaches.

Number Seven

Number Seven people enjoy the good life and they love to dine out, have nice holidays and buy good clothes and other possessions. They can be great fun, because they have outgoing and cheerful natures but there's a certain level of self-indulgence within them and an assumption that the world owes them a living. They usually manage to find the money they need to finance their lifestyle. These people manage to say the right thing at the right time to the right people and they can delight an audience with their wit and repartee. They dislike confrontation and arguments and they may be too insecure to stand up for themselves. Their innate sense of style can take them into the fields of fashion or entertainment where their good looks and meticulously chosen outfits are set to impress others. These people often look younger than their years. They fall in love quite easily but they can become bored and wish to move on fairly quickly but they may not know how to say this. Many Number Seven types prefer to remain single but if they do marry, it's unlikely that they will be faithful or stick with the same partner.

Oddly enough, despite the pleasure loving and apparently light-hearted nature of the Number Seven personality, they often work in fields that require a good deal of financial acumen and a strong sense of responsibility. These may include banking, savings and loans specialists, accountants, stock-controllers, mortgage brokers and so on. More obviously, the entertainment industry, arranging sports fixtures, public relations or running a smart restaurant, hotel or club. Lecturing and even mildly medical or therapeutic fields might appeal.

The health weak spots are the colon and bowels and also the chest and breasts. The hips and cranium are susceptible to injury.

Number Eight

These people are hard workers whose meticulous attention to detail assures that all their tasks are properly performed, but sometimes this attention to detail makes them lose sight of the larger picture. Slow, thorough, single minded and determined, these people get the job done. If their business ventures fail or if they lose their money, they are able work their way back up and to make a second or even a third fortune later in life. These folk move slowly and their calm exterior gives confidence to others but they can be weaker inside than they let on. They sometimes find it hard to make a decision and they can lose faith in themselves at times of stress. Their calm exterior and apparent lack of emotion can lead them into counseling careers and their strong moral views can lead them into becoming active in human rights or matters of ecology. The conservative Number Eight types don't accept change readily. In love relationships they are the type who enjoy a quiet and stress free family life. These people can be a great support to their loved ones but they need the security of a loving and supportive marriage in order to be happy.

Career choices might include working in any kind of service industry and also manufacturing, farming, haulage and the provision of goods. Some will be drawn to the police or civil service or banking while others prefer to work in the fields of beauty, hair and cosmetics.

Health areas to be watched are rheumatic aches and pains, obesity, constipation; trouble with the legs or with the sinus and also depression and hypochondria.

Number Nine

These charismatic people enjoy the limelight and they get noticed wherever they are. They are great communicators who can inspire others and guide them through troubled times. They may be excellent salespeople and they can promote themselves well. Their strong sense of right may lead them into some form of religious leadership and they can become the spokesperson for a group. Others among the Number Nine group are just as happy to be one of a crowd. They are honest, they don't carry grudges and they may trust others a little too much because they don't understand hidden agendas or ulterior motives. These warm passionate people are not especially competitive but their attractive appearance, communications skill and ability to lift the spirits of others can take them far. There is a streak of vanity among Number Nine folk and they love to have the best clothes, a nice home and an impressive car to ride around in. They dislike bad manners and scruffy or sloppy people. They may expect too much of others and be a little disappointed, but in business or relationships, if something doesn't work out, they move on fairly easily. In love relationships, their romantic soul means that they express emotion well. They draw others to them quite easily but they need to develop some discrimination about their choices of partner. They can become arrogant and fickle but they stick to a lover while the affair is going on and then move on and put the whole thing behind them. Adaptability is the name of the game for Number Nine folk, whether in work, relationships or life in general.

Career options might include the entertainment industry, the media or also customer relations, selling, public relations and marketing. Politics might appeal, as would the media, journalism and photography. Team building, networking, socializing and conducting an orchestra could be appropriate. Basically any job that requires the Number Nine person to think on his feet and to cope with a number of different things at once is suitable. Variety is the spice of life in any job for this type.

Chapter Four

The Elements

Character, Talent and Potential for Success

Another area of character reading is the Elements, and the Chinese people consider these to be extremely important. This chapter shows the character and talents of the various elemental types.

Now, find the elements for your month number and "magic square" number in the following table, and see how they fit you. They may well show different sides to your personality.

Number	Element
1	Water
2	Earth
3	Wood
4	Wood
5	Earth
6	Metal
7	Metal
8	Earth
9	Fire

The Elements and the Numbers

Each element can be assigned to one or two numbers, as you will see from the previous table.

The Wood Element

Three and Four

Wood people are the scholars of the Chinese zodiac, so if you have a Wood number among your three numbers, this will explain an aspect of your character.

Wood people have high standards, strong morals and ethics and they often have a strong belief in themselves. They have natural sense of the value of everything and they know instinctively what will work for them, and this can lead them into executive positions in their chosen careers. These subjects can attract others to their cause. In business, they like to join forces with others in order to create large-scale operations that encompass a variety of different products or facets, because focusing on one product or service bores them. Wood people flourish in a corporate environment, and they know how many beans make five, but they can expand too far, take on too much and thus find it hard to control either their business or their personal lives.

These folk are co-operative and considerate towards others and they are compassionate, caring and generous to others, but they aren't good at keeping money by for a rainy day. When times of trouble come around and they need themselves need help, they are astounded to discover that others are not as happy to return their generosity or kindness, as they were to give it.

Wood people gravitate to work in computing, electronics, science, communications and education. Either they receive educational opportunities at a young age or they seek out training and education for themselves later on. Some are idealists who try to improve the lot of others, but they may also be unrealistic or unworldly. Many are intellectuals who prefer to use their minds than to work with their hands, although some are inventors, and others work in some form of transportation. Many wood people are interested in religion, spirituality or philosophy.

The Fire Element

Nine

Fire people are the warriors of the Chinese zodiac, so if you have a Fire number among your three numbers, this will explain an aspect of your character.

Fire folk may become members of the armed forces, the police, the fire service and the ambulance service. They might be explorers, rangers, part time military people, adventurers, bandits and even travelers in space. They are comfortable with the technology of their times, but they put it to practical use rather than invent and explore on an intellectual level. Other fire types are to be found in show business, acting, entertainment or sports, but they may also be politicians and union bosses. These people want to be seen and to be known. While they may be idealistic when fighting for a cause, they are also personally ambitious. They are confrontational, short-fused, courageous and sometimes reckless. They can also be cruel and unfeeling. Some Fire types become top criminals!

Fire people are the leaders of the pack. They make excellent military leaders because they are decisive, courageous and self-confident, but they can go too far and become aggressive and reckless. These people are creative, they have some good ideas, and they can rally others to their cause, but they may forget that not everyone is as addicted to risk-taking as they are. They love movement and change, and their restless natures mean that they are never still for long.

Fire people can gamble, either in the literal sense or by taking chances in business or in life. They love a challenge and they tend not to see pitfalls before plunging ahead. These dynamic, pioneering, impulsive and outspoken folk certainly get things moving, but they can make enemies and they can be the architects of their own downfall. They may be impatient, irritable and hard to live or work with, but if they didn't exist, the world would not have progressed and developed very far.

The Earth Element

Two, Five and Eight

Earth people are the conservators of the Chinese zodiac, so if you have an Earth number among your three numbers, this will explain an aspect of your character.

The Chinese see the Earth element as being the center of their world, so it represented the Emperor and his court and the center of the known world. It stands for conserving the power-base and keeping things pretty much as they are. The image might be of safety first perhaps.

Earth people excel at work in construction, manufacturing, food production, farming, ecology, veterinary work and medicine. They are very tuned into nature and they are also aware of large-scale trends. These people may also find work as food processors, chefs, caterers and hotel managers. They usually do well in their chosen professions. Some own a farm or business, while others rise to an executive position in a large organization. They prefer to stay put and develop something than to move around much or change direction very often. They are sensible, reliable and realistic. Their nature is placid, slow to anger but also slow to forget a hurt. They have excellent brains and they can be shrewd in business.

Earth people are practical, methodical and organized and they create the solid foundations upon which any enterprise is built. These people make excellent executives, administrators, farmers and accountants and they have a firm grip on what will and what will not work. They can foresee trends and they have a talent for large scale and long-term planning, all of which makes them excellent government and civil workers, lawyers and bankers. Earth people are generous and loving to their families and their relaxed manner makes for a pleasant home atmosphere.

The Metal Element

Six and Seven
Metal people are the celebrities of the Chinese zodiac, so if you have a Metal number among your three numbers, this will explain an aspect of your character.

Metal people are creative and artistic, so they will gravitate to the arts. They can be found working as fashion or photographic models or they may be part of the entourage that runs around looking after the models, their make-up, hair and the rails of clothes. They may work in dancing, poetry, writing, composing, sculpting, acting, classical, rock and other forms of music and the media. Alternatively, they may manage people who work in those fields, or they may look after the places where things are displayed or where events take place. They may be associated with discos and nightclubs. Many metal people collect art, crafts and antiques, or are associated with galleries, museums, opera houses, theatres and so on. They may be film or television actors, or they may work in that field. Another possibility is to become the kind of newspaper or magazine journalist who follows celebrities around and writes about them.

Metal people may be amusing hangers-on, socialites and "wannabes" who have the time and money to be seen around in all the best places. They may have been born rich, or they rise in status through luck or good management. In short, these people turn their artistic, creative or managerial talents to good use through a combination of hard work, focused ambitions and plain good luck. Many are charming, witty, good looking or just plain lucky - as we in the west would say, born with a silver spoon in their mouths. Even here, the metal theme seeps through!

Metal people have determined and independent personalities and they are hard to influence. Once they have decided upon a course of action, they stick to it. This tenacity ensures that they can often turn a slow-starting enterprise into an eventual success but the downside is that they find it difficult to let go of a situation once it has become untenable. Their desire to have their own way stands them in good stead, as long as their vision of what will succeed is right, but it can lead to disaster when their hunches are off-center. These people don't brook interference even when it's meant kindly, and their supreme independence means that they prefer to handle problems by themselves. Metal people often have a good grasp of financial matters.

The Water Element

One
Water people are the logistics experts of the Chinese zodiac, so if you have a Water number among your three numbers, this will explain an aspect of your character.

In the ancient Chinese courts, Water people were the accountants and record keepers. They also directed such things as the transport of goods and people across the country, so they were in tune with current and unfolding events in a way that those who work in the stock exchange are now. Water folk have excellent commercial brains. However, they are also found in the world of the arts, media and creativity.

These are intuitive people who can spot a trend before it arrives, but they are also happy to encourage others to use their talents to good advantage. Water people live in a world of creativity and ideas, but they are also practical because they have the knack of turning ideas into concrete reality. Their intuitive talent for hitting on the right idea at the right time, and coupled with their salesmanship, this ensures that they can create a market when none existed before. Water people know how to find the right contacts and avenues for success and they can find ways of making things work for them. However, they dislike direct confrontation and they will always look for way round difficulties rather than to face them head on. These people can be bullied at times and they can make the mistake of leaning too heavily on stronger personalities. They do learn to stand up for themselves in time.

Today, water people tend to work in banking, finance, foreign exchange, the stock markets and home loan departments, along with credit schemes, insurance and so forth. Some are cashiers or bookkeepers and others are bookmakers. They may raise money for a cause or handle money on behalf of others. They know how to make money when times are hard. If they lose money, they usually find a way of making it back again. Despite their considerable financial skills, water people are gentle souls who like to help others. Some are artistic or creative and many of them enjoy music and dancing. Many put on weight in later life if they are not careful.

A very Chinese way of viewing matters related to water is that of communications, because the original method of transporting goods or of keeping in touch with others was to travel down the river and canal systems. This element is linked to all forms of communication and also with the movement of goods from one place to another. It links with marketing, sales, working in the media and also with keeping in touch with friends and family.

Chapter Five

The Elements: A Quick Prediction Method

This chapter shows you how to use the Elements to give a brief glimpse into any year or month that you wish to study. It also suggests ways of making the best of the prevailing situation.

You need to go through the system in the same way that you did to find your own Year and Month Numbers, but this time you must find the numbers for the year and month that you wish to check out, rather than your own, personal, Year and Month numbers.

To save you from having to go back to the front of the book, I've repeated the sequence, here but without the examples.

Finding the Year Number

Look at the following chart to find the year you wish to look up, and then track upwards to the number at the top the column in which your year appears. Remember that if you wish to check out any date before the solar New Year, which occurs on February 4, you must consider it as the previous year. For instance, February 1, 2013 would count as the year 2012.

YEAR NUMBER TABLE								
9	8	7	6	5	4	3	2	1
1901	1902	1903	1904	1905	1906	1907	1908	1909
1910	1911	1912	1913	1914	1915	1916	1917	1918
1919	1920	1921	1922	1923	1924	1925	1926	1927
1928	1929	1930	1931	1932	1933	1934	1935	1936
1937	1938	1939	1940	1941	1942	1943	1944	1945
1946	1947	1948	1949	1950	1951	1952	1953	1954
1955	1956	1957	1958	1959	1960	1961	1962	1963
1964	1965	1966	1967	1968	1969	1970	1971	1972
1973	1974	1975	1976	1977	1978	1979	1980	1981
1982	1983	1984	1985	1986	1987	1988	1989	1990
1991	1992	1993	1994	1995	1996	1997	1998	1999
2000	2001	2002	2003	2004	2005	2006	2007	2008
2009	2010	2011	2012	2013	2014	2015	2016	2017
2018	2019	2020	2021	2022	2023	2024	2025	2026

Finding the Month Number

To find the Month Number, look for the Year Number among the numbers at the tops of the three columns below:

MONTH NUMBER TABLE			
BIRTH DATE	1. 4, 7	2, 5, 8	3, 6, 9
February 4 to March 5	8	2	5
March 6 to April 5	7	1	4
April 6 to May 5	6	9	3
May 6 to June 5	5	8	2
June 6 to July 7	4	7	1
July 8 to August 7	3	6	9
August 8 to September 7	2	5	8
September 8 to October 8	1	4	7
October 9 to November 7	9	3	6
November 8 to December 7	8	2	5
December 8 to January 5	7	1	4
January 6 to February 3	6	9	3

The Elements and the Numbers

Each Element is assigned either one or two numbers as you can see in the table below. Therefore, if you are checking out a year that has the number 4 and a month that has the number 7, you will need to read the sections on Wood and Metal from the list below.

NUMBER	ELEMENT
1	Water
2	Earth
3	Wood
4	Wood
5	Earth
6	Metal
7	Metal
8	Earth
9	Fire

Wood - numbers three and four

It's time to think and to take a broad view of things, looking at them from all ways round rather than focusing on one narrow area of life.

Fire - number nine

Be enthusiastic, courageous and energetic. Stand up for yourself and fight for what you think is right. Develop leadership skills and take charge of others. Trust in your own instincts.

Earth - numbers two, five and eight

This is a time for stability and for building for the future and to behave in a slow, steady and practical manner. Take care of household and family affairs. Build up your savings and don't waste money or possessions unnecessarily.

Metal - numbers six and seven

Have fun. Treat yourself to something fashionable and attractive to wear or for your home. Visit glamorous or interesting places and mix with high status people. Visit a gallery, go to a show or take part in a parade. Also, be very determined to stay on your chosen path and to achieve your ambitions.

Water - number one

Look after the finances and take advantage of trends and opportunities that come your way. Don't be confrontational now because you won't win. Keep in touch with others and ensure that you cultivate those who will help you to get on in life. Appreciate that your intuition is increasing at this time.

Chapter Six

Preparing an Annual Prediction

This is the complex part of The Flying Stars system, but if you take it slowly and work through the examples, you will find it easier than it looks.

Overleaf, you will see a series of squares, each of which is divided into nine smaller squares. The smaller squares are called Houses and the numbers within the Houses are called "The Flying Stars", because they "fly" around the system as you use it - as you'll see in a minute.

Start Here
1. Find the year that you want to examine in the Year Number Table overleaf, track to the top of the column and make a note of that Year Number.
2. Look at the following Squares overleaf, and find the one with the Year Number that you want to examine in its *center*.
3. Now look in that Square for your own personal Year Number and make a note of its *house position* in the Square. For instance, someone might wish to look at a number 9 year, which would mean that they look at the Alpha square, because it has the number 9 in the middle. However, their own personal Year Number might be 2, so they make a note that the House that contains their Year Number is to the right of the center on the Alpha square.

YEAR NUMBER TABLE								
9	8	7	6	5	4	3	2	1
1901	1902	1903	1904	1905	1906	1907	1908	1909
1910	1911	1912	1913	1914	1915	1916	1917	1918
1919	1920	1921	1922	1923	1924	1925	1926	1927
1928	1929	1930	1931	1932	1933	1934	1935	1936
1937	1938	1939	1940	1941	1942	1943	1944	1945
1946	1947	1948	1949	1950	1951	1952	1953	1954
1955	1956	1957	1958	1959	1960	1961	1962	1963
1964	1965	1966	1967	1968	1969	1970	1971	1972
1973	1974	1975	1976	1977	1978	1979	1980	1981
1982	1983	1984	1985	1986	1987	1988	1989	1990
1991	1992	1993	1994	1995	1996	1997	1998	1999
2000	2001	2002	2003	2004	2005	2006	2007	2008
2009	2010	2011	2012	2013	2014	2015	2016	2017
2018	2019	2020	2021	2022	2023	2024	2025	2026

ALPHA		
8	4	6
7	9	2
3	5	1

BRAVO		
7	3	5
6	8	1
2	4	9

CHARLIE		
6	2	4
5	7	9
1	3	8

DELTA		
5	1	3
4	6	8
9	2	7

ECHO		
4	9	2
3	5	7
8	1	6

FOXTROT		
3	8	1
2	4	6
7	9	5

GOLF		
2	7	9
1	3	5
6	8	4

HOTEL		
1	6	8
9	2	4
5	7	3

INDIA		
9	5	7
8	1	3
4	6	2

4. Now, look at The Magic Square below and find the number in the same *House* that your Year Number occupied in the previous square. For instance, in our example the House was to the right of the center. In this case, the House contains the number 7. Make a note of this number.

THE MAGIC SQUARE		
4	9	2
3	5	7
8	1	6

5. Check out the nature of the year you want to look at in the interpretation that follows in the next chapter.

Tip box

The Magic Square is called Magic because, if you add up the numbers in any row, column or diagonal, they always total 15. You may notice that The Magic Square is also the same as the **Echo** square.

The good news is that once you've done all this, you only need to move down one number at a time to check out the following year, or go up one number to look at the previous one. Therefore, if you are in a Year 7 now, last year was a Year 8 and next year will be a Year 6. Technically speaking, that means that the numbers or stars "fly" around the squares.

Example
Work your way through this example and you will get the idea very quickly.

Emma wants to look at her prospects during 2014:

1. Emma finds 2014 and looks at the top of the column to find the Year Number for that year. It's 4.
2. Emma finds the square that has 4 in the center, which is Foxtrot.
3. Emma's own personal year number is 7 (because she was born in 1984). She finds the Number 7 on the lower left hand corner on the Foxtrot Square.
4. On The Magic Square, the lower left hand corner is numbered 8, so she reads about an 8 year in the text that follows.

YEAR NUMBER TABLE: 1900 - 2017								
9	8	7	6	5	4	3	2	1
1901	1902	1903	1904	1905	1906	1907	1908	1909
1910	1911	1912	1913	1914	1915	1916	1917	1918
1919	1920	1921	1922	1923	1924	1925	1926	1927
1928	1929	1930	1931	1932	1933	1934	1935	1936
1937	1938	1939	1940	1941	1942	1943	1944	1945
1946	1947	1948	1949	1950	1951	1952	1953	1954
1955	1956	1957	1958	1959	1960	1961	1962	1963
1964	1965	1966	1967	1968	1969	1970	1971	1972
1973	1974	1975	1976	1977	1978	1979	1980	1981
1982	1983	1984	1985	1986	1987	1988	1989	1990
1991	1992	1993	1994	1995	1996	1997	1998	1999
2000	2001	2002	2003	2004	2005	2006	2007	2008
2009	2010	2011	2012	2013	2014	2015	2016	2017

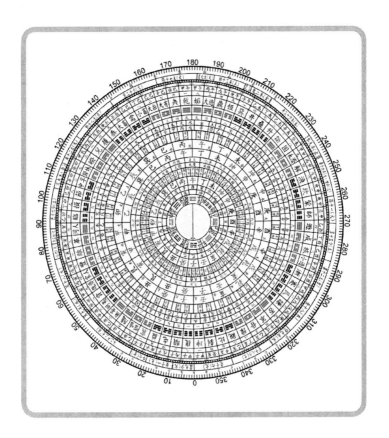

Chapter Seven

The Interpretations

This section gives predictions for the year ahead. Later, I will show you how to find the prediction for any month that you want to look at.

Each number starts by listing the Element, Season and Direction, the Key Ideas and the Image. The Season shows the time of the year that will be most important, while the Direction will show you which direction to go in for luck, money, love, improved health or whatever else you are hoping for. The Key Ideas are self-explanatory.

The Images are linked to ancient Chinese rural life. The majority of people in China worked on the land, so these images were familiar to them, and they became a kind of shorthand or easy reference to the activities and atmosphere that are linked to each House.

House One

Element: Water
Season: Winter
Direction: North

Key ideas
Nothing much happens now
Retreat and reflect
Rest, socialize and plan for the future

The Image

The dark, cold, wintry, northerly feeling of this House suggests a time of retreat and reflection, sitting in front of the television and not bothering to go out much. However, farmers the world over like to socialize, go to the theatre or cinema, eat with friends at restaurants and have parties during this quiet time. In the West, Christmas, Hanukah and other celebrations occur during this time. A rural image would suggest a time when nothing is growing and the animals are not yet breeding, but the farmer is cleaning, mending, sharpening his tools, replacing or updating worn ones and making plans for the coming year.

Interpretation

In personal terms, this signifies a time of withdrawal and a time to plan your future. Money may be in short supply and there's little opportunity for movement or expansion in your affairs. In Chinese divination systems, the element of Water doesn't denote the flow of feelings and emotions as it does in Western systems but the flow of business and finance. This iced up phase suggests that this is a time to count what money you have and to make a sensible budget or even to arrange loans to see you over this lean period.

You may push people away or you may withdraw emotionally from relationships or friendships. Caution, nervousness and even fear can characterize this House. You may suffer ill health during this period. If you are stuck in a job that you don't find satisfying, don't try to find something else, because you'd only find yourself back in a similar situation somewhere else. If a relationship is dying, you will be aware of the fact but unable to improve things or hasten its end.

You appear to be immobile but you can use this time to make plans and to set targets for yourself. The best course of action is to research or find the information you will soon need in preparation for the next phase of your life. Your plans will depend upon your personal circumstances, but you could use this period to gain a qualification or study something that you've always wanted to learn.

A more pleasant image might be of sitting by the fire, reading and resting. However, there's still a level of frustration at the lack of opportunities and a lack of movement in your affairs. Your best course is to stay put and to do everything you can to learn what needs to be learned so that you are primed and ready for action when times change. A positive side to this period is that your intuition will increase, and if you follow it, you won't go too far wrong. It might be a good idea to take up some kind of alternative or stress-relieving activity such as Tai Chi, yoga or meditation. On the other hand, in the West, this time of the year is when rural people socialize and have fun, and there's no reason to suppose that the rural Chinese are any different.

Water is a fluid, so health problems associated with the blood; lymph drainage system, bladder and even the reproductive organs might arise at this time. You should try to avoid environmental hazards, such as being caught in a flood or a blizzard or being out on a mountain when mist and cloud descend. It would be worth checking over your household appliances or working machinery and fixing or replacing worn out apparatus. If you are living or working in a damp and cold environment, you should get away from this if you can. Only drink alcohol within sensible limits.

If your own personal Year Number is 2,5,8 or 9 you will feel the restrictions and hardships even more keenly.

House Two

Element: Earth
Season: Early autumn
Direction: South west

Key ideas
Consolidate and build on what you have
Not much change, other than a possible house move

The image
The Earth element and early autumn feel to this House suggests that a calm phase is in operation. A rural image might be of a farmer resting after the harvest is in.

Interpretation
You may find that nothing much changes during this period and that your life is on a steady course. This is an excellent thing if you are happy with your lifestyle, but if you are itching for change, it won't come along yet. If you try to force change, you will only irritate and alienate others as well as driving yourself crazy with frustration. This is a good time in which to clear up outstanding jobs, to clear out cupboards and make space for new things. It's also worth analyzing your workload, so that you can off-load tasks that are no longer necessary. If you have certain habits or behaviors that are not good for you, this is a time to work on changing them. Any developments that occur now will move slowly.

Depending upon your personality and your personal situation, you may become depressed about the lack of movement in your affairs. Alternatively, you may boast about the happy state of your finances and your great lifestyle. The Earth element suggests that this may be a time to make minor improvements to your property or land, but it would be best to consolidate what you already have rather than to expand. However, you may actually move house or move your business at this time, and such a change would turn out to be lucky and beneficial.

Health problems are likely to be few, but swellings in the glands due to infection are possible, as are stones or fibroids forming somewhere in the body. The pancreas and spleen may give trouble. You will definitely need to take some exercise during this period.

If your own personal Year Number is 1,3 or 4, you will find this period more difficult than others will.

House Three

Element: Wood
Season: Spring
Direction: East

Key ideas

Get moving and make a start
Push hard for what you want
Don't move so quickly that you miss important details

The image

Everyone feels better when spring arrives, especially if the winter has been particularly hard. The sap rises in the trees and you feel that you are coming back to life again. The rural image is an obvious one, as this is the start of the farming year when plants sprout and animals give birth. Another image is that of the sunrise and the dawn of a new day.

Interpretation

On a personal level, ideas and inspiration will flow and your creative juices will be stimulated. Luck is with you now and you can bring luck and inspiration to others. This is the time to get large enterprises off the ground and to break out of the mold. Anything can be initiated now, and this might include a move of house, the start of a relationship, getting involved in politics, opening a business or pushing for promotion at work. This is also a good time for travel and speculative ventures, so you can afford to take an occasional gamble now.

The only real danger is of moving so quickly that you neglect something vital or miss some important detail. Your energy level will be high and you want to get on with life, but you might move a little to fast for safety. You could also overreach yourself in other ways, by tiring yourself out or even by giving yourself high blood pressure as a result of all the extra stress that you put on yourself. However, you can get in shape now, and if you want to take up some exercise or a sport, this is the time for it. You will have the energy and motivation to do this but you must take things slowly at first or you will damage yourself.

As far as health is concerned, your liver or gall bladder might become overloaded, so avoid eating fatty foods, very sugary foods or eating too late at night. It's worth going on a sensible diet, which means eating good food in the right kind of quantity, as that will help you to look and feel better.

Those with personal Year Numbers of 2,5,6,7 or 8 should try to avoid being too impulsive or bumptious.

House Four

Element: Wood
Season: Late spring
Direction: South east

Key ideas
A very busy and successful time
Market yourself, don't be a shrinking violet
Take time to rest and to think things over

The image
This is a time of rapid growth and advancement. The rural image is one of crops growing at a furious pace and animals

becoming fat and healthy. The weather is improving, although it's still a little cool and wet at times. The feeling is one of optimism. The sun rises higher in the sky and everything is warming up.

Interpretation

In personal terms, you should go after whatever it is that you want, as there's a momentum that will push all your enterprises towards the goal of success. If appropriate, pregnancy might be on your agenda. Whether your mind is fixed upon business, financial matters, personal relationships, domestic matters or anything else that you want, a little effort now will pay off very quickly. Indeed, the energy and optimism of this House reminds me of that famous Shakespeare quotation, "There is a tide in the affairs of men, which, taken at the flood, leads on to fortune."

This is the time to market yourself or to market any goods or services that you have to offer, because your ability to communicate will be especially effective. Give yourself a makeover and brush up your social skills so that you will become more attractive to others. If a better job or a promotion is in the air, you must do your best to be noticed in just the right way. In business, you must go after contracts and opportunities and be ready to expand. It should be easy for you to raise a loan if you need one. Advertising, judicious use of the media and putting the word around will be invaluable now. You can help your cause by taking on some kind of public speaking, lecturing or broadcasting in the media that serves the purpose of drawing attention to your product or service. You need to keep in touch with all the right people and to court important people.

As always, you shouldn't go at things like a bull at a gate, and you must guard against overdoing it. Be sure to avoid running out of money, strength or steam. If you fail at all during this phase, it will be due to a lack of courage, a negative attitude, lack of common sense, going at things too quickly without first doing your homework, or some other self-induced problem.

Health problems are likely to arise from overdoing things, so take time out to rest. Play games, go to the park and play with your lover and your children, take exercise and relax your mind and body. Respiratory or stomach ailments are possible, particularly colds and flu that result from getting cold and wet. Take off a few days here and there to rest, relax, retreat and reflect and to go over things in your mind. This will allow you time to review things and to spot those things that might give trouble later on.

Those with personal Year Numbers of 2,5,6,7 or 8 should take care to rest and not to overdo things during this phase.

House Five

Element: Earth
Season: The change of seasons
Direction: Center

Key ideas
One phase ends and another is yet to begin
If there are too many options, narrow them down
Seek balance in your life

The image
The ancient Chinese compass shows the cardinal angles of north, south, east and west, but also the center. The idea is that after each trip away, you always return to the center, so this phase represents returning after a journey or coming to the end of a particular phase. Now you can assess what you've gained or achieved, work out whether you enjoyed the previous period or not and prepare for the next one.

The image is of the changeover from one season to the next. In every Chinese system that I've come across, this change-of-season period is considered unpredictable and even dangerous. The danger here is not so much personal as financial, in that unreliable weather can affect crops or animals. The rural image is of getting one crop in and starting to plough for the next. Alternatively, of watching grapes grow, but all the while, hoping the weather won't suddenly turn bad and ruin the crops. Very hot, cold, wet or dry weather can affect young plants, while sudden storms, or weather changes that bring pests or diseases can ruin crops that are progressing towards harvest time.

Interpretation

In personal terms, this is a time of fluctuation and transition. Now is the time to look back over what you've done, to measure your progress and also to look forward to the future with all its possibilities and uncertainties. There may be too many options open to you and you may be faced with too many choices. Alternatively, you may have too much going on in your life, so that you are worn out much of the time and unable to do justice to any of it. There may a karmic reckoning to be faced at this time or karmic benefits to be reaped. Perhaps one side of your life is taking too much precedence while other aspects are being neglected, so balance is the thing to aim for. You need to strike a balance between what you do for others and what you do for yourself. You may need to search for a middle road between the demands of your family, your job and your own needs.

This is not likely to be a year of major change for you personally, but you will be in the center of everything that's going on around you. There are times when you will feel as though you are in the eye of the hurricane. Having said this, you may be tempted to start new projects or to make important journeys during this phase, but the advice is to think deeply before doing any of these things. Holiday travel is fine but anything more ambitious might be best left for another time. You may wish to look back to bad times in the past and perhaps speak out about past hurts, or you may wish to apologize to someone who you have hurt.

Despite the inner urge to push forward with your plans, your situation is so unpredictable that it's hard to say whether you'd succeed or not. Therefore, the message here is to tread water and to keep calm, because nothing can really be relied upon at such times. However, even if you are determined to do nothing other than to keep on a steady course, things might change of their own volition. Unexpected events could derail your plans or even throw your life into turmoil, and you may have to deal with a great deal of upheaval, commotion and confrontation. If this happens, you will need to strive for balance amid rapidly changing circumstances.

On a more positive note, you may find new ways of handling old situations. The strong emphasis on the center (represented by the element of Earth) means that your home or premises could become a center of activities. This might mean that you start to work from home or that your home becomes the center of social activities or you move to a more social location. Alternatively, you may set up a professional center, such as a health center or an arts and crafts center. You won't have to travel far because the world will find its way to you - possibly via the Internet. Another change that could come your way now is an unexpected change in your relationships, so if you are lonely at the start of this period things might well have changed by the end of it.

Serious health issues may arise, especially if these have been building up for some time past. Expect a visit to the dentist this year and don't take any health matter lightly. You may suffer from emotional ups and downs, not only in respect of your own experiences of life, but partly in response to the things that are going on among the people and in the circumstances around you.

Those with a personal Year Number of 1,3 or 4 will feel the most uncomfortable during this period.

House Six

Element: Metal
Season: Early autumn
Direction: Northwest

Key ideas
A time of achievement and success
Business travel and communications succeed
Don't become boastful
Avoid silly accidents

The image
The rural image is that the harvest is starting for some crops, while the remaining crops swell and ripen. Some animals can be sold or slaughtered and preserved now. The wind is turning slightly to the north and there are a few cooler days mingled with the hot ones.

Interpretation
In a personal sense, this is a time of prosperity and achievement, and even if this has not yet arrived, it soon will. This is a good time in which to take control of your life and especially of your business affairs. Business travel will be a success, but whether you travel or not, you will feel pleased with your efforts. Those in positions of authority over you will think well of you.

The danger here is of becoming arrogant or boastful or to believe that things will always be this good. The element of Metal always suggests determination and a disinclination to listen to what others have to say. If your situation is comfortable, happy and successful, you may be so pleased with yourself that you become convinced that your ideas are the only ones worth listening to, and that others have nothing useful to offer. This may work for a while but it could put the first few nails in the coffin of relationships with others at work or in your personal life. You may try to force your opinions on to others and you may become too dogmatic and demanding. Take care not to pick fights at work or at home, even if you think others are doing everything wrong. Try to enjoy this period of success and prosperity without letting your achievements and success go to your head.

An altogether more pleasant aspect of a Metal year is that you may become involved in something entertaining, such as the arts, dancing, singing, amateur dramatics, fund-raising, sports, fun-runs and so on.

You will feel fit and strong, so you may take on too much or rush at jobs too quickly and without sufficient preparation, thereby opening up the risk of accidents. Care must be taken when handling machinery or when traveling, and any injuries must be treated immediately. Health problems might come from injuries, especially to the head.

If your personal Year Number is 3,4 or 9, you might become so full of yourself or allow yourself to become so aggressive that you alienate others.

House Seven

Element: Metal
Season: Autumn
Direction: West

Key ideas
Have fun and splash out a little
Don't get into debt
Enjoy flirting, love and sex, but be careful

The image

The rural image is of the revelry after a harvest. The crops have been sold, the barn is empty, the stock is doing well and selling well, market prices are good and there's milk, honey and a glass of cider all round.

Interpretation

Everything you've done in the past has paid off and you can afford to rest and to take a holiday. This is the time to spend some money on your home and garden and to treat your friends and loved ones to something special. Avoid spending everything you have or living on credit or you will find yourself short when the wind begins to blow in the other direction once again.

Your sex drive will be high, and whether this turns out to be a good or a bad thing depends upon your personal circumstances and your natural tendencies. At worst, lust could encourage you to fall in love with someone who is bad for you or you may become obsessed with someone who doesn't really want you. You might even end up hurting others as a result of following up on a stupid attraction.

Health matters arise through dental and bone problems. Accidents are possible, as are colds that turn to bronchitis, also damage to the large intestine.

If your personal Year Number is 3,4 or 9, take especial care not to become boastful, alienate others or to take loved ones for granted because you will need their support when life becomes difficult once again.

House Eight

Element: Earth
Season: Early winter
Direction: South east

Key ideas
Life may be muddled
Avoid taking frustration out on others
Conserve time and money

The image
The rural image describes this as a quiet time when little is happening, interspersed with sudden storms that send the farmer out to check on his stock or his crops. This is a time of extremes, because either nothing will happen or everything will happen at once. Your life may fluctuate between these two points while this House number is in operation.

Interpretation
This House is called stillness by the Chinese and this reflects the stagnant feeling that may come over you at times during this period, but there will also be times when you are in the middle of great turmoil and unable to get much done. One image that fits this House would be the after-effects of a change of address when you sit in the middle of a great deal of muddle with little time or money to spend on putting things right.

You may feel stagnant or impotent in some way, and periods of frustration are bound to occur. You may find yourself living or working among strangers or you may push those who are familiar to you away from you. It seems as though your normal points of reference are out of kilter. Nothing will ride along smoothly because total stagnation is followed by everything happening at once and vice versa. The greatest problems come from misunderstandings, so be clear about what you mean and avoid dealing with those who can't or won't understand what it is that you want or where it is that you are coming from - or wanting to go to for that matter.

Health issues might involve the circulation system or bone and joint problems. You could be the victim of violence, possibly due to others becoming impatient with you because they see you as being uncommunicative and unresponsive to their wants and needs.

If your personal Year Number is 1,3 or 4, you will become particularly frustrated during this phase.

House Nine

Element: Fire
Season: Summer
Direction: South

Key ideas
A time of optimism and good health
Forge ahead with plans
Become a star

The image
The ancient Chinese loved the summer, because the crops and animals were doing well and they and their families were healthy and happy. To them, this period represented a time of achievement. The only downside was that a period of drought or high winds could cause problems.

Interpretation
On a personal note this House position represents fame and fortune, a time of acclaim, success and achievement of ambitions. If you want to take full advantage of this period, go all out for success and ensure that your name is the one that's put forward. This is a time of optimism and expansion, and you should take every opportunity for advancement that

comes your way, because you can put your message across successfully now. Even if you don't have a career or a job as such, you can make personal achievements and become a star within your own circle. Whatever your personal ambitions might be, you can achieve them during this phase, and you will receive the recognition and acclaim that you deserve. Anything you want to achieve should be within your sights now.

The only drawback is that you might overreach yourself and you will irritate others if you become obstinate or boastful. Your increasingly public image means that you will have to behave very well, because if there are any skeletons in your cupboard, this is when they will emerge.

There is no reason to suspect that you'd be ill during this time, but you should try to balance your work and social life with rest and some gentle exercise. There may be many calls upon you, and you may need to be here, there and everywhere, so you must learn to turn some of these invitations down in order to preserve your strength. The Fire element of the year could bring sudden fevers, burns, accidents, eye problems and heart or circulation problems. Take care when dealing with tools or machinery or when cooking or dealing with hot things of any kind.

If your personal Year Number is 1,6 or 7, you may not be as happy or healthy as you should be during this phase.

Chapter Eight

Monthly Predictions

Just as you can look at the prospects for a particular year, so can you also look up the prospects for a particular month, and this chapter shows you how.

Tip box

This is a repeat of the technique that I showed you at the start of this book, but it saves you from having to go back through the book to work it out.

1. If you've already worked out which year you want to look at, make a note of its Year Number.
2. If you haven't, then you need to go back to Chapter One and find it.
3. Now find the column in the following table that has the Year Number among the numbers at its head.
4. Find the date that you want to check out and track along to find the corresponding Month Number in the relevant column.

MONTH NUMBERS			
BIRTH DATE	1,4,7	5,2,8	3,6,9
February 4 to March 5	8	2	5
March 6 to April 5	7	1	4
April 6 to May 5	6	9	3
May 6 to June 5	5	8	2
June 6 to July 7	4	7	1
July 8 to August 7	3	6	9
August 8 to September 7	2	5	8
September 8 to October 8	1	4	7
October 9 to November 7	9	3	6
November 8 to December 7	8	2	5
December 8 to January 5	7	1	4
January 6 to February 3	6	9	3

The Squares and the Houses

Now we use the same system again that we saw in the previous chapter:

1. Find the square that has the Month Number that interests you in its middle.
2. Locate your own personal Year Number on that Square.
3. Look at The Magic Square and find the number that occupies the House that your Year Number is in.
4. Now, look up that number in the Interpretations chapter. (Chapter Seven).

You will see an example of this in action, in a minute.

ALPHA		
8	4	6
7	9	2
3	5	1

BRAVO		
7	3	5
6	8	1
2	4	9

CHARLIE		
6	2	4
5	7	9
1	3	8

DELTA		
5	1	3
4	6	8
9	2	7

ECHO		
4	9	2
3	5	7
8	1	6

FOXTROT		
3	8	1
2	4	6
7	9	5

GOLF		
2	7	9
1	3	5
6	8	4

HOTEL		
1	6	8
9	2	4
5	7	3

INDIA		
9	5	7
8	1	3
4	6	2

THE MAGIC SQUARE		
4	9	2
3	5	7
8	1	6

Example:

1. Alex wants to look at his situation in the middle of March 2015.
2. He was born in 1977, so his year number is 5.
3. He finds the number 5 at the top of the middle row of the Month table.
4. He finds that most of the month of March, including the bit he's interested in is Month Number 1.
5. He finds the square that shows Number 1 in the center, this is India.
6. He finds his own personal Year Number at the top middle house of India.
7. He looks at the Magic Square and finds that the top middle House is Number 9.
8. He goes back to the previous chapter and reads about Number 9 in the interpretation section.

Chapter Nine

Ideas Linked to the Elements

This chapter goes into a few ideas associated with the elements and numbers within the Flying Stars system. When you get to the part about lucky numbers, check out the situation for your Year Number, Month Number and Magic Square Number.

The Elemental Seasons

If you intend to start a job or an enterprise or to enter a new phase in your relationships, it's useful to know the element that's in charge during that time. Remember that the Oriental year starts in February, so the elemental seasons work as shown in the following table.

THE ELEMENTAL SEASONS	
February:	Earth
March:	Wood
April:	Wood
May:	Earth
June:	Fire
July:	Fire
August:	Earth
September:	Metal
October:	Metal
November:	Earth
December:	Water
January:	Water

Lucky Numbers

Every one of us has a Year Number, but this is shared with everyone else who was born in your year. The Month Number is a bit more individual, as it isn't the same for everyone born in the same month. Indeed, the Month Number varies according to the Year Number and the date of birth. However, the number that's truly individual is the Magic Square Number (see Chapter Two).

You can use the lucky and unlucky numbers for anything from lotteries to check out the number of an address, a car number or the number on your office door or the address of your workplace or anything else that has a number. There is no guarantee that a lucky number will bring you exactly what you want, so try the system out for yourself and, if you get good results more often than half the time, then that's much better than flipping a coin!

If you want to check out an address or a car number, it's likely to have more than one number in it, so you must reduce these to one by adding them together.

Examples:

➤ 52:   5 + 2 = 7
➤ 764:   7 + 6 + 4 = 17
   (Seventeen is not a single digit, so we reduce it again).
➤ 17:   1 + 7 = 8
➤ 4587:   4 + 5 + 8 + 7 = 24
   (Twenty-four is not a single digit, so we reduce it again).
➤ 24:   2 + 4 = 6

The Lucky Number System

Number One
➤ Lucky numbers: 6 and 7
➤ Fairly lucky numbers: 3 and 4
➤ Neutral number: 1
➤ Unlucky numbers: 2, 5, 8 and 9

Number Two
➤ Lucky numbers: 5, 8 and 9
➤ Fairly lucky numbers: 6 and 7
➤ Neutral number: 2
➤ Unlucky numbers: 1, 3 and 4

Number Three
➤ Lucky numbers: 1 and 4
➤ Fairly lucky number: 9
➤ Neutral number: 3
➤ Unlucky numbers: 2, 3, 6, 7 and 8

Number Four
- ► Lucky numbers: 1 and 3
- ► Fairly lucky number: 9
- ► Neutral number: 4
- ► Unlucky numbers: 2, 5, 6, 7, 8

Number Five
- ► Lucky numbers: 2, 8 and 9
- ► Fairly lucky numbers: 6 and 7
- ► Neutral number: 5
- ► Unlucky numbers: 1, 3 and 4

Number Six
- ► Lucky numbers: 2, 5, 7 and 8
- ► Fairly lucky number: 1
- ► Neutral number: 6
- ► Unlucky numbers: 3, 4 and 9

Number Seven
- ► Lucky numbers: 2, 5, 6 and 8
- ► Fairly lucky number: 1
- ► Neutral number: 7
- ► Unlucky numbers: 3, 4 and 9

Number Eight
- ► Lucky numbers: 2, 5, 8 and 9
- ► Fairly lucky numbers: 6 and 7
- ► Neutral number: 8
- ► Unlucky numbers: 1, 3, and 4

Number Nine
- ► Lucky numbers: 3 and 4
- ► Fairly lucky numbers: 2, 8 and 9
- ► Neutral number: 9
- ► Unlucky numbers: 1, 6 and 7

Lucky Colors

The Flying Stars system links each number to a color, and you can use this system when you need a boost to your confidence. You've plenty of colors to choose from, as you can select one from your Year Number, your Month Number or your Magic Square Number, or you can use something from all three.

LUCKY COLORS	
Number One:	White or silver
Number Two:	Black or dark blue
Number Three:	Bright green
Number Four:	Rich dark green
Number Five:	Yellow
Number Six:	White
Number Seven:	Red
Number Eight:	White
Number Nine:	Dark wine red

Chapter Ten

The Flying Stars and Feng Shui

Now we look at The Magic Square in a different light, as each number relates to a different area of life.

THE MAGIC SQUARE IN FENG SHUI		
4 Prosperity	9 Recognition	2 Relationships
3 Elders	5 Health	7 Children
8 Study	1 Career	6 Friends

You need to draw a rough sketch of your house, flat, room, business premises or farm, with the doorway or entranceway that you habitually use facing the front.

Now draw the Magic Square on some transparent paper and put it over your house sketch.

This is how it will look:

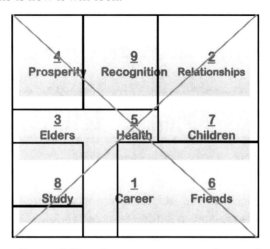

Draw a diagonal line from one corner of your house or workplace and then draw a second one that links the other two corners, and take note of where they cross. The crossing point will be the middle of the premises, which is the health area.

The following is a very brief way of making the best of your location from the point of view of Feng Shui.

One

Career prospects: Improve your career prospects by keeping this area neat and tidy. If your hallway is long and narrow, break up the swift-moving Chi by hanging some chimes up or by placing a semi-circular table at the side. A picture of an animal facing the front door or an ornament of an animal placed so that it can look out of a window will keep bad Chi out. Anything made of Metal will help your career prospects, so a metal framed picture or mirror or a metal object would be worth placing near the front door.

Two

Relationships: Put a picture of your lover in this area. Keep this area calm and attractive by adding pleasant colors and plants in pots.

Three

Ancestors and family: A picture of your parents, grandparents, in-laws or other relatives will aid your current relationship. A picture of one who has passed on will help invoke his or her help from beyond the grave. If you have a bad relationship with your parents or in-laws, this might actually help to improve the situation.

Four

Prosperity: Hang some of those Chinese coins that you can buy in tourist shops here. Alternatively, put three, six or nine ordinary coins on a shelf or in the corner closest to the outside of the house. Water will help the flow of communications so put a water-feature ornament that has moving or flowing water here if you want to communicate with others.

Five

Health and strength: Even if other areas of your home are untidy, try to keep this area clear and avoid placing anything dirty here. Dirty cups, ashtrays and so on should not be allowed to sit around in this area. If a toilet occupies this position, move house, because you will become ill in a house like this.

Six

Gods, religion, friends, helpers and travel: Hang pictures here, of your friends or of places you'd like to visit. If you like religious statuettes or pictures (any religion or spirituality), or if you wish to make a household altar, put all these things here.

Seven

Children, creativity: A nice ornament here will help to keep your relationship with your children sweet. If you want to be productive, something related to the element of fire will help; so put an attractive red candle here.

Eight

Study, contemplation: The obvious thing to keep here is a bookshelf, but you might also want to put a filing cabinet here. Otherwise, use this for magazines and even the television.

Nine

Recognition, esteem: Buy an Oscar statuette from a gift shop and place it here. If there's any other symbol associated with your search for respect or fame, put it here.

After dealing with your house as a whole, go over each room individually. Hold a piece of paper with bottom of The Magic Square facing the wall where the entrance is. If something is out of kilter in your life, put something appropriate and optimistic in the representative room. For instance, if you work from home, place some coins in the money area of your workroom or if you are looking for love, place a romantic picture in the Number 2 position.

Finally, if your home is an irregular shape with an area of the Magic Square that falls outside your house, put a mirror on the wall with its back to the missing area, as this will bring the missing part into play.

Chapter Eleven

Weighing the Bones

Now for something really different!

Bone Weighing seems to come from the same roots as the Flying Stars and Chinese astrology. The Chinese use the words bones or skeleton in the same way that we would say roots or foundations, so these bones could be called the roots of the system. The technique is easy to use and the readings that follow it could be classified as quaint. The system does seem to work, but as with any other divinatory system, you should make up your own mind whether or not you place any credence on it. This method of fortune telling doesn't require you to get on the scales in order to weigh your bones, because you only need to use the simple tables given below to discover your "bone" weight.

About the only drawback to this system is that the hour of birth is used. Like many other Chinese systems, the day is broken into two-hour blocks, so this gives some leeway in cases where the exact time is not known. You should use local time at the place of birth, but you will need to deduct an hour for British Summer Time or for Daylight Saving, if necessary

According to tradition, the "heavier" your bones the more likely you are to have a healthy, wealthy, stable life and plenty of happiness, but those whose bones are light will have more interesting if less stable lives, while the lightest bones of all have dreadful lives with no luck at all.

Technique

1. Consult the tables to find the weight of your bones for your year, month, day and time of birth. The weights are given in ounces and decimals of ounces. This may sound tricky, but the system is really very easy.

2. Add the weights of your bones for your year, month, day and time of birth together, to discover their total weight.

3. Once you've found your weight, look up the reading.

Tip box

The year table begins at 1924 and ends at 2020. For births before 1924, add 60 to the year. For births after 2020, deduct 60 years. This gives you a figure within the range of the table.

Example one: 1910 + 60 = 1970

Example two: 2025 - 60 = 1965

You'll find two examples of weighing the bones for a person at the end of the lists of tables.

Table of Weights for the Year of Birth

1924 - 1.2
1925 - 0.9
1926 - 0.6
1927 - 0.7
1928 - 1.2
1929 - 0.5
1930 - 0.9
1931 - 0.7
1932 - 0.7
1933 - 0.8
1934 - 1.5
1935 - 0.9

1936 - 1.6
1937 - 0.8
1938 - 0.8
1939 - 1.0
1940 - 1.2
1941 - 0.6
1942 - 0.8
1943 - 0.7
1944 - 0.5
1945 - 1.5
1946 - 0.6
1947 - 1.6
1948 - 1.5
1949 - 0.8
1950 - 0.9
1951 - 1.2
1952 - 1.0
1953 - 0.7
1954 - 1.5
1955 - 0.6
1956 - 0.5
1957 - 1.4
1958 - 1.4
1959 - 0.9
1960 - 0.7
1961 - 0.7
1962 - 0.9
1963 - 1.2
1964 - 0.8
1965 - 0.7
1966 - 1.3
1967 - 0.5
1968 - 1.4
1969 - 0.5
1970 - 0.9

1971 - 1.7
1972 - 0.5
1973 - 0.7
1974 - 1.2
1975 - 0.8
1976 - 0.8
1977 - 0.6
1978 - 1.9
1979 - 0.6
1980 - 0.8
1981 - 1.6
1982 - 1.0
1983 - 0.7
1984 - 1.2
1985 - 0.9
1986 - 0.6
1987 - 0.7
1988 - 1.2
1989 - 0.5
1990 - 0.9
1991 - 0.7
1992 - 0.7
1993 - 0.8
1994 - 1.5
1995 - 0.9
1996 - 1.6
1997 - 0.8
1998 - 0.8
1999 - 1.0
2000 - 1.2
2001 - 0.6
2002 - 0.8
2003 - 0.7
2004 - 0.5
2005 - 1.5

2006 - 0.6
2007 - 1.6
2008 - 1.5
2009 - 0.8
2010 - 0.9
2011 - 1.2
2012 - 1.0
2013 - 0.7
2014 - 1.5
2015 - 0.6
2016 - 0.5
2017 - 1.4
2018 - 1.4
2019 - 0.9
2020   0.7

Table of Weights for the Month of Birth

January	0.5
February	0.6
March	0.7
April	1.8
May	0.9
June	0.5
July	0.6
August	0.9
September	1.5
October	1.8
November	0.8
December	0.9

Table of Weights for the Day of Birth

1 - 0.5
2 - 1.0
3 - 0.8
4 - 1.5

```
 5 - 1.6
 6 - 1.5
 7 - 0.8
 8 - 1.6
 9 - 0.8
10 - 1.6
11 - 0.9
12 - 1.6
13 - 0.8
14 - 1.7
15 - 1.0
16 - 0.8
17 - 0.9
18 - 1.8
19 - 0.5
20 - 1.5
21 - 1.0
22 - 0.9
23 - 0.8
24 - 0.9
25 - 1.5
26 - 1.8
27 - 0.7
28 - 0.8
29 - 1.6
30 - 0.6
31 - 0.5
```

Table of Weights for the Time of Birth

11pm to 1am	1.6
1am to 3am	0.6
3am to 5am	0.7
5am to 7am	1.0
7am to 9am	0.9
9am to 11am	1.6

11am to 1pm   1.0
1pm to 3pm   0.8
3pm to 5pm   0.8
5pm to 7pm   0.8
7pm to 9pm   0.6
9pm to 11pm 0.6

Example

The example that I've used here is for Hazel. She was born during the summer, but her time of birth comes within the same two-hour band with or without deducting an hour for British Summer Time.

Hazel

Year:	1965	0.7
Month:	August	0.9
Day:	21	1.0
Hour:	2.18 am BST (1.18 am GMT)	0.6
TOTAL:		**3.2**

Here is another example, for Stan. He was also born during the summer and during British Summer Time. His hour of birth also remains the same, with or without BST.

Stan

Year:	1968	1.4
Month:	July	1.6
Day:	31	0.5
Hour:	8.35 pm BST (7.35pm GMT)	0.6
TOTAL:		**4.1**

According to the list, both Hazel and Stan will have unstable but interesting lives with much travel, changes of career and possible changes of marriage partner. Let's hope that they are happy with their interesting lives - whatever happens.

An Example of the Best Reading That Could Happen

Year (1918 or 1978):	1.9
Month (April or October):	1.8
Day (18 or 26):	1.6
Time (9am to 11am or 11pm to midnight):	1.6
TOTAL:	**7.1**

Interpreting Bone Weights

2.2 Dreadful, a life of penury, coldness and struggling to make a living.

2.3 Drifting, abandonment, wandering and never finding a permanent home.

2.4 Nobody will love you, there will be nothing to achieve, a wasted life.

2.5 Exile, being excluded from a family, but things may look up later in life.

2.6 You start out alone and poor, but things improve later on.

2.7 Hard work with little help from others, but you can make it if you try.

2.8 You may be too unrealistic to make a success of your life.

2.9 The first half of your life is awful, but by middle age, things improve greatly.

3.0 Yours is a life of hard work and much travel.

3.1 You work hard when young and reap rewards when you are older.

3.2 You start out in a small way, but success builds slowly.

3.3 Travel and little success when young, but happiness and prosperity when old.

3.4 Yours is a religious or spiritual outlook.

3.5 Caution should be your watchword, as you are likely to be swindled.

3.6 If you work hard, nothing bad will come your way.

3.7 You will experience many difficulties, and money comes and goes.

3.8 Weak health and bad luck in youth, but 30 brings a turning point for the better.

3.9 It's hard for you to make a success of anything.

4.0 Tough, single-minded attitude pays dividends in the end.

4.1 You are a rebel when young, but more conservative later in life.

4.2 Life may be quite dull at first, but money and fame come later on.

4.3 You are soft hearted and a bit of a loser when young, but you learn much and gain money later.

4.4 Take life easy and don't kill yourself working, because success will come.

4.5 Peace is hard to find, but with support, you can fulfill your hopes.

4.6 Much travel and change; try to settle in a warm place.

4.7 A good life with many nice children, and money that flows in.

4.8 Work hard while young, to reap the rewards later on.

4.9 Friends will help you to build for the future. Success comes later.

5.0 A self-centered attitude when young, an improved attitude brings success later.

5.1 It takes a while for you to find the right way, and then happiness and success come.

5.2 Luck and an easy life.

5.3 You will always have money.

5.4 Plenty to eat, a good home and great clothes, as long as you are honest and hard working.

5.5 A slow start, then fortune smiles.

5.6 Intellectual and wise, you never stop learning. Much travel and many experiences.

5.7 A happy, easy life with good fortune.

5.8 Fame, fortune and a long life.

5.9 You will go far, travel and do well in life.

6.0 Education brings opportunities, wealth, honor, land and property.

6.1 Wealth, fame and honor.

6.2 Education, wisdom and intellect will take you far.

6.3 You will achieve something special and earn a place in history.

6.4 You will reach a position of authority and make lots of money.

6.5 A military life would bring honors. If you choose some other lifestyle, you can fight your way to the top.

6.6 A life filled with beauty, wealth and fortune.

6.7 You come from a good family, money surrounds you and it always will.

6.8 An up and down life with great success after a few wilderness years.

6.9 Wealth, fame, honor and pleasure will be your destiny.

7.0 You will reach the highest strata of society with wealth, fame and success.

7.1 Wealth, power, success and honors are yours to enjoy.

Conclusion

I am proud to announce that this book is the first in our new "Discover" series. These books will all be produced in paper and digital formats, as printed books, eBooks, DiskBooks, and various other formats as the technology develops.

Digital formats enable us to produce color-illustrated books, which up to now have been impossibly expensive for a small publisher in a niche market to produce. We overcame this problem with the "Simply" series, by joining forces with a much larger co-publisher, but the "Discover" series is ours alone.

If you are reading this in a paperback, and would like to try one of our eBooks / DiskBooks, visit our website (www.zampub.com), where you'll find all you need to know about these formats, and how to purchase them.

*****

Whenever I have gone about researching Chinese systems, I have always been stumped by the lack of information in English and the apparent complexity of the systems. However, I enjoy unraveling difficult concepts and making them easy for others to understand and use, and that's what I have done with The Flying Stars. I am now in the process of demystifying the Four Pillars system of Chinese astrology, so, if you've enjoyed this book, look out for one on that subject from Zambezi Publishing, sooner or later.

Index

Zambezi Publishing Ltd

We hope you have enjoyed reading this book. The Zambezi range of books includes titles by top level, internationally acknowledged authors on fresh, thought-provoking viewpoints in your favourite subjects. A common thread with all our books is the easy accessibility of content; we have no sleep-inducing tomes, just down-to-earth, easily digestible, credible books.

~~~~~

Please visit our website (www.zampub.com) to browse our full range of Mind, Body & Spirit, Lifestyle and Business titles, and to discover what might spark your interest next...

~~~~~

Please note:-
Our books are available from good bookshops throughout the UK, but nowadays, no bookshop can hope to carry in stock more than a fraction of the books published each year (over 200,000 new titles were published in the UK last year!). However, most UK bookshops can order and supply our titles swiftly, in no more than a few days (within the UK).

You can also find our books on amazon.co.uk, other UK internet bookshops, and on amazon.com; in the USA, sometimes under different titles and ISBNs. Look for the author's name.

Our website (www.zampub.com) also carries and sells our whole range, direct to you. If you prefer not to use the Internet for book purchases, you are welcome to contact us direct (our address is at the front of this book, and on our website) for pricing and payment methods.

Lightning Source UK Ltd.
Milton Keynes UK
UKOW03f1612020913

216406UK00001B/2/P